RECYCLING

WE
RECYCLE

A TRUE BOOK

by

Rhonda Lucas Donald

Children's Press®
A Division of Scholastic Inc.

New York Toronto London Auckland Sydney
Mexico City New Delhi Hong Kong
Danbury, Connecticut

Plastic containers
wait to be recycled in
San Luis Obispo, CA.

Reading Consultant
Linda Cornwell
*Coordinator of School Quality
and Professional Improvement
Indiana State
Teachers Association*

Content Consultant
Jan Jenner
*Rendalia Biologist
Talladega, AL*

*Author's Dedication:
For Mom,
a champion recycler*

Library of Congress Cataloging-in-Publication Data

Donald, Rhonda Lucas, 1962–
    Recycling / by Rhonda Lucas Donald.
        p. cm.—(A true book)
    Includes bibliographical references and index.
    Summary: Explores the problems of waste disposal and ways to
reduce, reuse, and recycle to save resources and create less waste.
    ISBN 0-516-22193-0   0-516-27356-6 (pbk.)
    1. Recycling (Waste etc.) [1. Recycling (Waste)] I. Title. II. Series.
TD794.5 .D65 2001
363.72'82—dc21
                                                    00-057042

©2001 Children's Press®
A Division of Scholastic Inc.
Printed in the United States of America.
1 2 3 4 5 6 7 8 9 10 R 10 09 08 07 06 05 04 03 02 01

Contents

The Fresh Kills landfill lies on 5,000 acres of former tidal wetlands.

Waste Worries

The typical American throws away 4 pounds (1.5 kilograms) of garbage every day. That may be heavier than your backpack. In a year, all that trash adds up to nearly three quarters of a ton. That is almost as heavy as eight refrigerators! Multiply that by nearly 275 million Americans, and you can see why waste is a big worry.

What is in all that trash? Nearly half of it is paper. Grass clippings and yard wastes come in second, followed by metal, glass, plastics, food scraps, and other stuff such as clothing, wood, and rubber. Most of it ends up in landfills, huge holes in the ground where the trash gets dumped, crushed, and

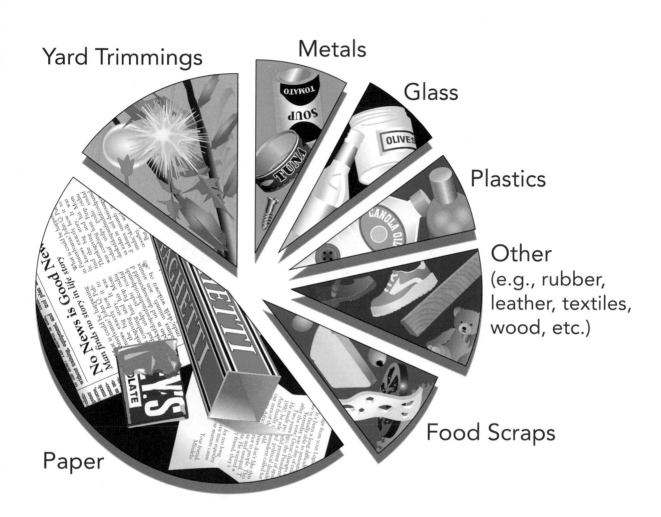

Yard Trimmings

Metals

Glass

Plastics

Other (e.g., rubber, leather, textiles, wood, etc.)

Food Scraps

Paper

This graph shows what is in our trash.

buried. Some landfills are so big that they are like mountains. In fact, the community of Virginia Beach, Virginia, turned a landfill into a real mountain, which they named Mount Trashmore.

Unless we want to get buried under mountains of trash, we have to cut down on the trash we create. Landfills are filling up all over, and many communities do not want new ones. Landfills are

Seagulls fly around a mountain of trash.

smelly, dirty places. More seriously, sometimes toxic wastes in the garbage leak into the soil, polluting it and the groundwater. Besides, trash in landfills does not break down, or degrade. Because no air or sunlight can reach them, paper, food scraps, and other trash that would normally rot away to become part of the soil are not able to do so. Scientists who study landfills have dug up thirty-year-old newspapers that they could still read! Burning the trash in incinerators also causes trouble.

An incinerator puffs pollution into the air.

Incinerators create air pollution, and the leftover ash can be toxic.

A Trash Zapper

Atlanta, Georgia, scientist Louis Circeo has invented a way to turn garbage into something good. How? He uses a special torch that is hotter than the sun's surface (7,000° Celsius or 12,632° Fahrenheit) to melt the garbage. What is left cools off and turns into a clean, glossy black rock that can be used in buildings and roads. This "zapped" trash takes up a lot less landfill space. For example, a layer of garbage 10 feet (3 meters) deep can be turned into a layer of rock that is only 1 foot (30 centimeters) deep.

Why isn't everyone zapping their trash? Right now, the torch costs a lot of money to use. Someday, though, it may be the "hottest" way to get rid of garbage.

The Three Rs

Remember the three Rs that will trim down your trash: reduce, reuse, and recycle. You reduce by not buying stuff you will have to throw away later. Take a look at your lunch. If you pack a prepackaged meal in a paper bag, you will end up throwing

A lunch packed
in non-recyclable
containers.

away the plastic container,
the plastic covering over the
meal, and any "disposable"

spoons or utensils that came with it. If you eat prepackaged cookies or chips, there is yet another plastic bag in the garbage, not to mention the lunch bag.

If, however, you pack a sandwich in a reusable container, wrap an apple in a cloth napkin, and carry it all in a cloth bag or lunch box, there is nothing to throw away. Other ways to reduce trash include buying products

A lunch packed in reusable
or recyclable containers.

in large quantities (to save packaging), not buying throwaway things, and fixing broken toys or mending torn clothes instead of buying new ones. When you go shopping, look for items that have little or no packaging, or choose those packed in recyclable materials.

By using things more than once, you save resources and create less trash. Can you think of a new use for an old

T-shirt? If you cannot mend or pass on used clothes to someone else, tear them up and use them as cleaning rags. How about a plastic grocery bag? There are lots of ways to reuse plastic bags. You can carry things in them again and again before recycling them. They can also line trash cans or become the stuffing for hand-sewn pillows. When you shop, go to thrift, second-hand, or

Flea markets give people a chance to purchase and reuse old items.

antique stores instead of buying new things. Donate outgrown clothes, household goods, and other things you no longer need to charity so someone else can reuse them.

You probably know something about recycling. Hopefully you already recycle plastic, cans, glass, and paper at home and school. Nearly all of our trash can be recycled, but more people need to participate. Today, nearly one-third of the waste in the United States is recycled. What about the other two-thirds? We need to find ways to recycle things besides bottles, cans, and paper, too. Did you know you can recycle old tires? Motor oil? Even videotapes and computers? See the resources in To Find Out More on page 44 for more ideas about recycling beyond the curbside.

These teens are separating recyclables into different containers.

Recycling

Can you match these things made of recycled materials to what they were made from?

Match-up

Answers (clockwise from top): jacket/ plastic soda bottles, steel cans/steel scrap, stationery/old maps, road pavement/ glass, picnic table / plastic milk jugs, pencils/newspapers, picture frame/bicycle parts

Composting: It's for the Worms!

You can recycle food scraps, yard waste, and other organic garbage into soil-enriching compost. There are two ways to compost. One way is to put all your organic garbage into an outdoor bin. The bin need not be fancy—a piece of

A compost pile (above) can help plants such as this little red dogwood (inset) to grow.

chicken wire shaped like a barrel works just fine. The bin needs to have holes in the sides so that air can get in, and it needs to get sunlight.

Here is a recipe for compost. You mix "brown" stuff (dead leaves and branches, straw, sawdust) with "green" stuff (veggie peelings, grass clippings, green leaves and branches, weeds). You can also add eggshells, tea and coffee grounds, hair, waste from plant-eating animals such as rabbits and hamsters, and wood ashes. Things not to put in your compost pile include oils; animal products such as grease, fat, and bones; dairy products; or waste from meat-eating pets such as cats and dogs. Add enough water to make the pile damp but not soggy, and use a shovel to turn the

This family is adding compost to a container garden.

stuff over a few times. Turn the compost about once a week. If you smell an odor coming from the pile, turn it right away. In a month or two, you will have rich, dark compost ready to add to your yard or garden. Compost is a great all-natural fertilizer.

The second way to compost is the worm way. The best composting worms are red wigglers. You can order

Red wiggler

them and the bins to keep them in from companies that sell natural gardening supplies. Set up the bin by layering shredded newspapers about four inches deep in the bottom. Moisten the newspaper so that it is damp but not standing in water, and then add the worms. Add food wastes and kitchen scraps (see above for what not to add), then cover everything with

A worm wiggles among the "brown" stuff and the "green" stuff in a compost pile.

more shredded newspaper. Cover the bin, making sure air can get in, and keep it in a quiet place indoors. A pound (0.373 kg) of worms can eat about a half pound (0.187 kg) of waste per day. Check the worms every couple of days, and add water if the newspaper gets dry. Soon the paper and waste will vanish, and the compost will take their place. Scoop

How does compost work? Bacteria, fungi, worms, and insects, feed on the wastes. Their "left-overs" and droppings are "processed" garbage that helps make compost rich.

out the compost from the
top—being careful not to
scoop out any worms—and
add more newspaper and
scraps.

Do Not Dump It!

If you recycle as many things as you can and compost organic waste, you will find that there is not much left to throw away. There are some things, though, that you cannot recycle, reuse, or compost, and you must dispose of them properly. For example, paint,

These things are hazardous wastes that must be disposed of safely.

paint thinners, nail polish and remover, batteries, some glues, and pesticides are toxic trash that you should never dump down a drain or throw into the trash. The chemicals in toxic trash can seep into the ground and get into water, polluting it. To get rid of toxic trash, call your local office of solid waste. Most communities have special drop-off sites, or they will collect toxic materials at certain times during the year.

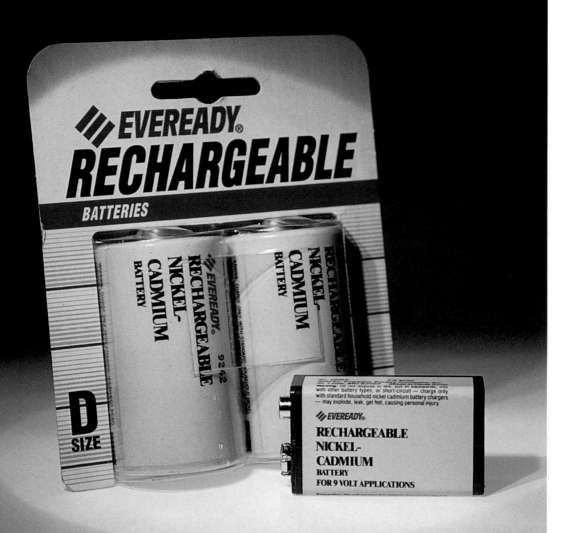

Rechargeable batteries are not only reusable, but they also reduce hazardous waste.

Try not to buy things that will create toxic trash. Avoid using pesticides, for example, by practicing natural gardening ways that discourage pests—such as putting ladybugs in your garden to eat unwanted bugs. Buy rechargable batteries, and buy only enough paint for a single project. Always look for products that are non-toxic. The fewer toxic things we use, the better it is for everyone.

Ladybugs are natural pest controllers.

To Find Out More

To learn more about recycling, check out these resources:

 **Books**

The EarthWorks Group. **50 Simple Things Kids Can Do to Save the Earth**. Andrews and McMeel, 1990.

The EarthWorks Group. **The Recycler's Handbook.** EarthWorks Press, 1990.

Gibbons, Gail. **Recycle: A Handbook for Kids.** Little, Brown, and Company, 1992.

Schwartz, Linda. **Earth Book for Kids: Activities to Help Heal the Environment.** The Learning Works, 1990.

Woodburn, Judith. **Garbage and Recycling.** Gareth Stevens Publishing, 1992.

Organizations and Online Sites

City Farmer
*www.cityfarmer.org/
wormsup179.html#worm
supplies*

This site lists sources of composting worms for many U.S. states and Canadian provinces.

Cornell Composting
Department of Agriculture and Biological Engineering
Riley-Robb Hall
Cornell University
Ithaca, NY 14853-5701
*www.cfe.cornell.edu/
compost/schools.html*

Just about anything you might want to know about composting you can find here—even weird and unusual composting.

Environmental Protection Agency (EPA)
Public Information Center
401 M St., SW (TM-211B)
Washington, DC 20460
*www.epa.gov/epaoswer/
osw/kids.htm*

The Kid's Page of the EPA's Office of Solid Waste has recycling information, games, and activities. You can also join the Planet Protectors Club and get free stuff.

Kids Web
King County
316 3rd Ave.
Seattle, WA 98104
1-800-325-6165
*www.metrokc.gov/dnr/kids
web/solid/buyrec*

The Natural Resources Kids' Page on Solid Waste and Recycling lists lots of products made from recycled materials.

Operation: Landfill Elimination
*www.geocities.com/
RainForest/5002/index.html*

This site lists more ways than you can count to reuse and recycle just about anything.

Important Words

compost also known as "humus," a nutrient-rich part of soil made of the remains of living things

degrade (also biodegrade) break down naturally over time, becoming part of the soil. Organic wastes degrade if exposed to air and sunlight.

groundwater underground water in pockets of soil and rock that supplies fresh water to about half the people in the United States

incinerator a device that burns trash at very high temperatures

landfill huge hole in the ground lined with plastic where trash is dumped, crushed, and finally buried under the soil

organic describes things that were once alive and can break down naturally over time

toxic poisonous

Index

Meet the Author

Rhonda Lucas Donald has written for children and teachers for fifteen years. Her work has appeared in magazines such as *Ranger Rick* and *Your Big Backyard*.  She specializes in writing about science and natural history and creating projects that make these subjects fun. Rhonda received the EdPress award for best newsletter of 1997 for *EarthSavers*, an environmental newspaper and activity guide. She has also written several other environmental True Books for Children's Press. She lives in North Carolina with her husband Bruce, cats Sophie and Tory, and Maggie the dog.